WTF?!?

Where's the Faith?

Steven M. Hartwell
Foreword by Alvernis Johnson

HMG Publishing
Saginaw, Michigan

C. J. Loray Productions, Inc.
Editor
Saginaw, Michigan

Cover Design: The HMG Agency
Saginaw, MI

Author Photo: Suite 211 Photography
Detroit | NYC | Worldwide

Dedications

I would like to dedicate this book to my lovely beautiful wife, L'Oreal Hartwell, also to my children Matthew, Hannah, Morgan, Hailey and Zoe! The love I have for you can never be erased. My dear sweet wife, I thank you for your patience, your wisdom and your grace. You are such an elegant lady, who possesses poise and dignity. You are such a class act. I am privileged and honored to fall deeper in love with you everyday.

Table of Contents

ACKNOWLEDGEMENTS

A Special Thanks to my Grandmother, Easter Gibbs, and my Grandfather, John William Gibbs, who have instilled in me Christian values and taught me how to depend on Christ for everything. Thank you for hammering in me a solid work ethic that will forever be with me, which is something I can pass down to my children. My love and respect for you is never-ending. I love you, Granny and Paw Paw. :-)

I would like to thank my parents, Hudie and Delores Langston, for your continued support and love. To my sweet Mother, you are such an example to me. The testimony you have on how you overcame is phenomenal! I take my hat off to your accomplishments, becoming one of the first women in our family to achieve her Master's Degree and will be the first Doctor in our family. Also, to my sister, Equina Hartwell, for being there whenever I needed you. You are definitely Lori's and my best friend. I Love You!

Thank you to all who supported this project. My staff members who helped bring this project from my head to a physical product! Thanks to Missy Powell on staff web developer, and Donna T.

for the Audio. A special thanks to my Mother-In-Law, Clarice Johnson, of C. J. Loray Productions, Inc., for all the editing and proofreading. Thank you for putting up with my numerous calls and questions. I wasn't an easy client. However, you handled it with grace and poise!

I would like to give a special thanks to two very special people in my life, Alvernis and Shantell Johnson. You two have imparted so much into my life. Thank you for the late night talks, the advice and for never giving up on me! To my Dad, Alvernis, thank you for encouraging me to become more, even when I felt I was inadequate and not prepared enough. Thank you for making me feel like I could achieve anything. Thank you for the talks we had in the car on our way to Walmart. I appreciate you for your never-ending wisdom that is truly a gift from God!

Thank you to a host of others that have helped, encouraged and uplifted me.

FOREWORD

I have had the distinct pleasure of knowing Steven Hartwell for more than fifteen years. I remember the first time I saw him sitting in the audience at one of our church services in Saginaw, Michigan at Kingdom Life Ministries. I knew right away that there was something unique about him. He wore success like a pair of well-fitted gloves and his posture was indicative of a man with great purpose and promise. At the conclusion of the service, I greeted Steven as I normally did all our visitors. I had no idea that, what seemingly started out as a causal encounter, would soon blossom into a solid father-son relationship. Steve, he was at the height of his professional career. He was a very enterprising young man with a passion that was completely unbridled. If there was ever a "Go-Getter," it was Steven. His cell phone was plastered to his ear like air to the wind. Just barely in his twenties at the time, he was producing at an award-winning status. As matter of fact, as I recall, he was one of the youngest persons to own his own company in the industry. I watched this young man grow into a wonderful husband, great father and leader.

All of this did not happen overnight, nor did it come easy, however. I remember when Steve first shared with me his love interests in my niece, L'Oreal. At the time, she was a young college student studying at Michigan State University. I was sure of two things – one, that he would make her a great husband and two, she would not be interested. I told Steve to let me play "Cupid" and see what his chances were. The next time we gathered for family dinner, I casually mentioned it to L'Oreal, and she seemed a bit reluctant. However, just a little while later, she seemed opened to the idea. Today, years later, they are one of the happiest couples I know. Together they are raising five beautiful children and setting a pattern for their generation. Their ability to navigate through the trials of life can only be attributed to their great faith. They have weathered incredible storms and have risen above the waves of trouble like skilled surfers manipulate the tidal waves.

In this riveting literary work, Steven takes you through a candid look at his most turbulent times and how he overcame them. His transparency is refreshing as he takes you into the intimate, and sometimes embarrassing, moments of this very personal journey. This writing is sure to encourage the most challenged individual, as well as strengthen those who have chosen faith as a way of life. You'll see firsthand how faith works and how important it is to keep it at the forefront of your life. Once you get past the shocking title and plunge into the content of the pages of this book, you will be sure to find invaluable principles that will help you discover true faith. Life throws curves at all of us and there are times we feel helpless. We've all had those days that we wondered, "What is really going on?" I know I have asked the questions many times, "God where are you, and why is this happening to me?" In order to get the right answers you must ask the right questions. I encourage you today not to search for why a thing happens, but rather ask yourself, "Where is my faith so that I can get through it?" Steven does a great job at helping you answer that question. I know, as you read this book, you will be blessed and your faith will accelerate to new heights. Read, Believe, and Become!

Alvernis L. Johnson

#INTRODUCTION

It was a cold, burly morning, but it was not totally winter yet. It was just enough coolness to know old man winter was putting on his hat, his overcoat and his furry gloves to make his annual arrival on the east coast. I remember waking up thinking, "Dang, is this really my life?" At this time in my life, I was living in a hotel room with my wife and family sleeping beside me. My oldest son was two years old and my youngest daughter was two. But, did I forget to mention? My wife was pregnant with twins! I woke up in this hotel room at the age of 29 thinking, "Can this really be my life?"

We had just lost everything we had! That is why we were living in a hotel. We had lost our beautiful home. I lost my thriving business, along with my confidence. I was so perplexed. I thought I had done everything right. Although, I am no perfect guy, I did not think I had done anything to deserve this. It was very frustrating. Even though I had a relationship with God, I remember being so confused!

Not really knowing what to do, I would rely on weekly sermons from my local church to try to figure life out. To be totally honest, I felt even more confused. I was not getting the warm and fuzzy feelings anymore, like when I would hear weekly sermons from my pastor. No disrespect towards my church family, but deep down inside, I knew it was a personal journey for my family and I. We had to walk it out for ourselves.

Life sometimes can be so crazy, lame, unfair, stupid, sucky and just plain, outright cruel! There were times I actually hated lottery winners! They would walk in the store, spend a couple bucks on some numbers and they'd hit it big, winning sometimes up to hundreds of millions of dollars! I remember watching some lottery winners on news conferences celebrating their winnings and getting really upset because I knew I barely had more than $20.00 in my bank account. Many times, I had nothing, but loose coins. I thought to myself, "How unfair! I work so hard for scraps. You can come into the store, spend a few bucks and gain so much money it would take you two lifetimes to spend!"

When I look back at that time, it seems funny to me, now. I did not know those people, nor their story. I was just going off of assumption and pure jealousy. Well, I knew God had a plan. I was just tired of not knowing it. Reality hit when I laid in that hotel room with nothing. I had a decision to make. I could either succumb to my situation, or rise above it. I chose to rise above it! I wish I could tell you the moment I decided. I began to hear the "Rocky" theme song playing in my spirit. You would think, I'd get up every morning, hitting the pavement, feeling like a champion while running out the door, chugging down a glass of raw egg yolks. My wife, in her morning attire, would wait for me to kiss her as I charged out into the world. Sadly, that was simply not the case! Some days, I barely got out of bed. Depression began to set in because of my situation. Other times, I would walk out the door and my wife would be too busy with the kids to even notice I had left. Also, the part about the egg yolks…I say, "YUCK!"

I will share some tools I have learned to master a crazy, sometimes unfair, life. The greatest thing that brought my wife and me through some of life's craziest turns were our ability to believe! Our faith! Even though, when things looked bleak and dark, we still had a level of optimism in us to believe. I speak with all types of people every day. No matter who you are or what religious background you have, we all are victims of life's uncertain situations and circumstances.

However, through it all, we must keep our ability to belief intact. It is in that which we believe will be, is the most treasured thing that God has given us. So this book will help you on your journey to regain focus, grow your faith, and get back in the ring again! Dream bigger! Those of you who have lost faith, have the courage to believe again. I hope you not only heard my sincerity, but also the "Rocky" music playing! I'm just kidding about the music. In life's difficult, sometimes challenging circumstances, I want to ask you WTF???? Where's The Faith? Let's start believing again.

#TAKE ACTION

I have to admit, I love the nightlife! The definition of "Night Life" may be a little different from when I was a teenager, to where I am now with a wife and five kids. My nights used to consist of late night eating, hanging out with my friends, and acting stupid. Some nights would mean spending a night in jail for driving on suspended license. Boy, I was really dumb back then!

Let's fast forward to present-day. I have a wonderful wife and five beautiful kids. These days, my late night indulgences consist of celebrity news, blog reading, and watching Youtube videos. This particular night, while watching my favorite Ted Talks videos, I ran across an array of commencement speeches. It was like I had stumbled across a treasure chest of wisdom. There were speeches by Oprah, Michelle Obama, President Obama, and many more of the greatest Icons of our time.

One of my favorites was by a woman named Shonda Rhimes. She is a famous Hollywood writer, the brilliant creator of some of the top television shows of our time. Because I have a special love for writers, I was so intrigued by what she had to say. In her speech, she began to speak of some valid truths. However, what impressed me the most is when she stated that it's the 'doers' who are the ones who live their dreams. It's not the hippie daydreaming people, but people who go out there and make it happen. This struck a chord in me. There are many people out there who really hope to be successful and happy, but all they ever do is hope. They never graduate to the believing part.

When I was in school, I would always notice the kid who was left a grade behind. They were the biggest kids in the class. They would easily fill the entire chair as they'd be slumped over the small wooden desk. If the metal chair could speak, it would have been desperately crying out for help. The kids' voice would be deeper and he would quickly become the most feared because of his size and height. The kid failed to apply his skills and abilities to rise to his potential. He was unfortunately left behind to re-do another year in the same grade.

May I give you a powerful truth? You have the power to turn it all around. I think the most deceptive thoughts are that you cannot do it. It's too hard, you may say. This is the kicker, however, no one else is doing it like that! Let me give you the missing ingredient that separates you from the people who are fulfilled and happy. Are you ready? It's the doing part! Profound, isn't it? But, it's the secret that gets most people tripped up. They simply just don't get it. If it were simple, everyone would be at the top of their field. It would be the new normal.

The reason why so many people are not tapping into the good life, is some hope and then mistakenly call that faith. Others have works without any faith. Some people say, maybe I'll do it tomorrow. Those who hope makes up in their mind to go after their dream. They set a goal and say by this time next year or some other delayed date, only for it to come and go. Then there are those who work hard and commute to a job that they hate, however, they never step out and try to have more. You think that just because you don't have the degree the promotion requires, you won't apply for it, even though you deserve it. You don't even know what's waiting for you.

People have mastered how to become crisis managers. They only put action in when it is absolutely necessary. They set the compass of destination barely making it. This, unfortunately, is the norm of our society. But, I have a distinct feeling, if you're reading this book, you want more out of life. Not only in your finances, but you want the feeling of satisfaction and fulfillment. If that's not you, then I would humbly suggest that you do as Dr. Maya Angelou so eloquently conveyed, "When you learn, teach." It's only the doers that become the decision makers and world changers, not those who only dream.

How do you take action? When a negative thought comes to mind, it could totally take you off focus concerning your goal. You have to consistently and constantly override those negative thoughts by focusing on your immediate goal - to take action. I have been down this road before, thinking, "This will never happen for me." But, the moment I set a course to maintain my positive focus, those negative thoughts loses power and before I know it, it will only be a faint cry in the wilderness, so to speak. It literally becomes non-existent.

Everyone has to submit to the process. When I looked up the definition of what the word process meant, this is what I found: Process is a series of actions or steps taken in order to achieve a particular end.

I would marvel at the transformation of Hugh Jackman. I love anything that has anything to do with the movie "Marvel." When they launched the X-Men franchise, I was like a fat kid who died and went to a seafood buffet in the sky. I saw how his physical features were transformed from being Wolverine to his other parts in the movie, Logan and James Howlett. Then to see the appearance of his characters in other movies outside of X-Men, it's amazing how he can transform his body like that.

In an interview, he explained the grueling process he had to go through to get a body like that. It was not easy, but it was possible. He had to work out a couple times a day. He stated he ate many pounds of chicken, but it paid off in the end. The Wolverine franchise alone has made 100's of millions of dollars. Although, he had to submit to a process that got him those end results. If you want results you have to be willing to be a doer and submit to a process!

If you want to be successful in your career, find out who is successful in doing what you want to do. Research and study what their daily activities are and begin to build a blueprint to mimic them. Find out what process they had to take to get where they are. The most negative thoughts that comes to a person's mind is that it takes too long. However, you never realize the momentum you gain when you get a certain mindset to achieve something through small action steps.

I remember when I was a small child, I lived in a house that was at the end of the hill. My cousin, Tanika, and I would love to ride our bikes down that hill, and sometimes, our wagon. The process to get up the hill was not fun. It was very uncomfortable, at the time. On some days, it was very hot! So, we would start our journey uphill to enjoy the ride down. The walk started out slow. We would chat just to distract ourselves from the journey up that hill. Just before we would hit the peak, it would become the hardest, but we knew once we made it up there, we could enjoy the momentum the hill brought. We arrived up top and we would always pause to enjoy the scenery. We would also stop to take a break from the long uphill walk we had to endure. We would get on our bikes. As we took off downhill, it was exhilarating. The wind blew through our hair and all the work we had to endure was totally forgotten.

The truth I want you to extract is, once you get momentum behind you, it will not take as long as you think. You are thinking with an old mindset, which has gotten you to where you are today. Should you really trust it? Make up in your mind today that you are going to submit to the process of becoming a doer, a person of action!

#WHO CARES IF ROME WASN'T BUILT IN A DAY?

When we talk about taking action, many people cannot stay on task. I have heard many people say, "Rome wasn't built in a day." Have you ever heard that? I've heard it said many times when I was growing up. It wasn't until I got older that I understood this concept. When I did a little research on this phrase, this is what I have found:

The phrase, "Rome wasn't built in a day," is an adage attesting to the need for time to create great things.

People used this saying when referring to others who may be rushing to change some things or to implement new strategies to make changes in their different organizations, business or even their personal lives.

14

I am a nice healthy size person! Who am I kidding? I'm a real fatty! I love anything with grease. Before I started making changes in my diet, the closest thing to healthy in my diet was nuts. By the way, I like the nuts that starts out with dough in front of it. I remember I would get all fueled up by listening to Tony Robbins or by watching an Oprah special. On the show, she would have an inspiring guest who overcame an obstacle and would have obtained the ultimate prize of sitting down with the queen of Television, Ms. Winfrey. (By whom I secretly wish to be interviewed! Hey, it could happen.) I would have the feeling I could take this weight challenge seriously. Finally, I made up in my mind I was going to beat the bulge. I would wake up craving bacon and would go cold turkey from everything. I would go without everything: no sweets, no dairy, nothing. Then I would start my exercising by trying to jog like an Olympic runner. I would lift all 300 pound weights all in one day. Then, little by little, day by day, that resolve would fade slowly away. My moods would turn on me and what I used to do every day, became "I'll do it tomorrow." Then, I did it just two days a week. I convinced myself I could double up to make up for the lost days. Sounds familiar?

There was one key thing that I was not realizing, I was rushing the process! I started out with this great expectation of finally pushing through those negative emotions and triumphing over what was plaguing me. However, because my expectations were not set correctly, I was disappointed and lost enthusiasm. I slowly lost the belief that I could do it. When you are anxious about something, you will always miscalculate and not set your expectations correctly.

Have you ever set your alarm clock and when it went off you hit the snooze button until the very last possible minute to wake up? Then, you wake up rushing to get dressed only to make it to work, school, or to a meeting without that book, presentation, or the material you were going to have for the meeting? Your expectation made you think, "I can sleep until the last minute and be mentally prepared and have everything I need." You were, no doubt, disappointed, right? You may get away with it once or twice, but to live your life like that will be unfruitful. It's like gambling with your day every day, when you wake up.

It took 1,009,491 days to build Rome! Yes, that's a lot of time that it took. The reason why I entitled this section, "Who Cares that Rome wasn't Built in a Day," is because for one we're not in Rome, and for two, the Roman system of doing things, that is very outdated in the present time, I guarantee, it would have not taken that long!

I have been on the heavy side the majority of the thirty four years that I have been living. If takes me six months to a year, which is very possible, to lose this weight. That would not be a lot of time! Would it? Six months to a year compared to thirty four years is not long at all. So, what I did was just adjust my expectations and purposed not have that anxiety on my back to lose this weight by tomorrow! To everyone that's dealing with weight issues, wouldn't be lovely to be on the weight loss reality show, "The Biggest Loser", and lose two hundred pounds in one season on TV? Unfortunately, the majority of us have lives, businesses, and families that are depending on us. With this in mind, we have to take the alternative route. Without anxiety, I can have the freedom to find my own pace to run my life. This allows the freedom to maneuver my way correctly and find my own pace of doing things.

Deadlines are daunting and are as bad as they sound. When you have anxiety, your mind cannot even process correctly. Have you ever been chased any time in your life? Maybe you can remember being chased by your parents when you were little or the memory of being chased by a dog or an animal. You didn't even think about anything else, but I have to get away. You were driven on pure instincts! After the fact, you would replay the situation in your mind and realize what you could have done differently. That's how many people live their lives, with anxiety and stress. When you're in that state of mind, you cannot even think straight or properly to think of ways to deal with the situation.

I would advise you to slow down and think about areas of improvement that needs to be made. Think of areas where you allowed your expectations to falter and were not lined up correctly. Begin to attack these issues head on with the right mind ready to win this battle.

#STRATEGIES

I want to go into more detail concerning developing strategies. First, we need to understand how to be strategic! One of my favorite movies is "Ocean's Eleven." Matter of fact, I loved the entire franchise. If you have not seen any of them, you are missing out on a treat! It features many of the Hollywood heavy hitters. Its' like a gourmet feast of genius talent all in one movie!

I will not spoil it for those who have not seen it yet. But, I will say this much, the gist of the story is they are a bunch of thieves who manage to pull off some very genius heists in very methodical ways. The way that they planned these ventures is very entertaining and very ingenious! They spend a lot of time properly planning and executing their plans. It would not have been a global hit franchise if they just planned a job, then executed it. Everything would have been great and they would have gone home. The movie lights would have come on as the credits rolled. Ha!

I could just imagine the bickering from the crowds demanding their money back. I could imagine a geeky looking kid with glasses, bad acne and braces with his skin turning different shades of red, because of all the angry customers. Fortunately, it did not happen like that. It was entertaining because they had a many obstacles to overcome, when their plans were interrupted by unforeseen circumstances. I'm not condoning that you plan any robberies! This may have been a bad example, but it is my book! Just kidding. We can take a look at this movie and pay close attention to the wisdom that this movie brings.

When you set out to do something in life, you will have to become very strategic in what you accomplish! Think about it. Look around you - the house you live in, the car you drive, the clothes you wear, the medicine you see people taking - everything you see there was a strategic way for them to create it!

Someone had to sit down and think, how can I build a box that can keep things cold? Oliver Evans began to draft plans. Then, Jacob Perkins built the first compressor (the Refrigerator). They were very strategic in their approach to obtaining the goal of a refrigerator. This invention is being used all over the world!

If you plan on accomplishing anything in life, you have to have a strategic plan to reach the goal. You have to create milestones and have a willingness to stick to it. The reason why so many people have problems with sticking with a plan is because their plan lacks clarity. So, any resistance in that plan quickly diverts them! They waver in their commitment. When you have a clear direction and a strategy, those two become the ingredients that ignite results in your life. That's where focus comes in. I will deal with that a little more in an upcoming chapter. For now, lets get back to my "Ocean's Eleven" story. They encountered all kinds of situations in this movie. It was not the perfect heist, but with clarity and strategic forethought, they were able to accomplish a perfect score! When it is over, the payoff is always sweeter than the journey!

I am pretty sure as complicated as it was for the Wright brothers to build the airplane, the payoff was way better than the trial. Even though they had to face many trials and errors, they had to endure to see their vision come to life. Tyler Perry is one of my greatest inspirations, besides my dad, of course. Mr. Perry was homeless and slept in his car. He went belly up on more than one occasion. He worked in hotels, saved up his money to produce a theatrical stage play, only to open to an empty theater. He had to endure many things, to now being one of the most powerful forces in Hollywood. He is now worth a staggeringly amount of money. It is astounding.

I can go on and on about other examples of people who have made it. But, let's bring this home. Let's make this personal. If you or I want to accomplish anything, we must be strategic and always know that the end goal is always sweeter than the journey.

#THE POWER OF TWO - PURPOSE AND INTENTION

These two words, in this modern day, have been so overused. I know you have probably heard these two words used quite often. It can lose its potency when it comes to igniting passion that drives you to action. *Purpose* and *intention* are two of the most important forces you can have behind you when you want to make changes in your life!

Now let's break down these two components so that you can properly have them aligned, so that you can gain maximum impact in your life. The basic definition of purpose is why you do a thing. What is the true motive in your heart? Ask yourself, "Why do I do what you I?"

I remember, when I had set out to become an entrepreneur, I always struggled academically. Not that I was dumb or anything like that. The efforts of Academia never held my attention long enough for me to be interested. My brain always seemed to go into overdrive. It was just very difficult to keep my attention long. Did I have A. D. D. or something? Absolutely not!

I always dreamed of becoming my own boss. I was a dreamer. I've always dreamt of being the person who had all the answers. The one who whisked into the office everyday, with the wind flowing behind me, as I am tucking my super boss cape in the back of my suit coat! The phones ringing off the hook and everyone loving me! I hope as you're reading, you can pick up my hint of irony. I will give it to you straight! I wanted to become my own boss because I simply wanted to be rich. That was my purpose. I was a bull headed person and did not want to take orders from no one. That's the truth.

When I started out, I had the talent of problem solving, which came easy to me. In the mortgage industry, I prepared acquisitions. The closing of the deal was my favorite part. Many companies hated this part the most, because the closing of the deal is where all the problems would surface. Many principles involved would lose a lot of money if it did not all come together. I have seen people literally almost get into fist fights over huge acquisitions. But, I loved it. I enjoyed the challenges that awaited, putting my problem solving skills to work. I had a very high closing rate and was known as "The Closer" among my peers.

I am also a very strategic person and have been labeled methodical, at times. With these skills I possessed, I was sure to become a super boss. That was not the case, unfortunately. You see, a few years after I started a business of my own, the economy took a dramatic downturn. I was met with high rent for office space, a lack of new customers, and hardly no money for staff. At one point, I even had my sister in-law working for me. Business was bad! As a result of that, I got really depressed. My purpose, which was to become rich, was not strong enough to help me through the rough patches of this business venture. Sadly to say, my purpose was rooted in selfishness.

Even though I consider myself to be an awesome businessman, I have made some mistakes along the way. My focus needed to be corrected. I just want to make this disclaimer: even though I had the wrong focus, I have never allowed that to violate my integrity! I always remained honest and integral in my business dealings. During that rough period in my life, I was able to redefine my true purpose. I understood, as a business owner, I was able to help contribute to my community by offering a job to an unemployed person or donating to underprivileged children in our community. Having the resources, as well as, being able to network with other like-minded innovators was key. I was able to help provoke change in my community.

The number one game changer on what my purpose is: to bring inspiration to people to believe! I remember reading about so many stories about people who made great changes in modern medicine, and accumulated great wealth, starting with little.

One of my favorite shows is Million Dollar Listings. Josh Flagg is one of the stars on the show. His grandmother came to the United States with $2.50 in her pocket. She passed away this year (2014) and was worth a reported over a 100 million dollars! She accomplished great things. You have that same potential. You have that same greatness inside of you. It's time to reach your potential.

My heart longed to reach every person who is discouraged to let you know, you can make it! You can do it. I never wanted to be Tony Robbins, who is a great and awesome speaker, or Les Brown who is one of my favorite speakers. I just wanted to get my message out to as many people that needed it! I know what it is like to work a 9-5, barely making it! You're making just enough to get by. It's what I like to call the working poor! My wife and I both worked 9-5 jobs and it still was not enough to survive. Once I got my purpose in line, it gave me the boost I needed to keep going.

Whenever you start on something, your purpose can get lost. As you encounter great obstacles, always remember why you started out. You can accomplish great things if you do that. It became great for me after I started to question my purpose. It evolved and I began to mature. I was able to recommit to my initial intention. #Intention

I want to conclude this chapter on being a doer and taking action with one word. It's called *intention*. In my opinion, this is what so many people lack. When you set out to accomplish your goals, you get distracted and your true intentions get cloudy and murky in some ways! Have you ever got into a disagreement with someone and you forgot the initial reason for the conversation? It was never your intention to end up getting into a heated discussion. However, somewhere along the way, the intentions got murky. Tempers may flare up and things may escalate to something that was never a part of your plan. This happens all the time to people who set out to make change. Some are full of fire and passion. Things happen that weren't intentional and the initial intention gets lost. How can we prevent life from eagerly waiting by like a night stalker to steal everything you set out to accomplish? The answer is, we must always keep our intention clear.

What is the definition of *intention*? Intention, in its easiest definition, is a plan of action! That's it, in its basic form. You have to have a clear, precise plan of action if you want to succeed at changing things you want to see in your life. You must make your intentions clear. Well, you may ask, how can I apply that to my life? Life is sure to throw curve balls, and try to distract you from your intention or plan. If you allow yourself to become distracted, you will wake up years later wondering what happened.

You may say, "This was never a part of my intention or plan. I never planned to get pregnant at this age. I never intended to live paycheck to paycheck, drowning in debt, owing check advance places all over town. I never intended to raise my children on my own after my husband walked out on me." I can just see your inner man screaming, "This was not my intention!" So when life throws those curve balls, make sure you keep your intentions clear, and stick to the plan!

Now, how does *purpose* and *intention* work together? If you have the right type of "why" you do a thing, which is *purpose*, added to a good plan, which is *intention*; these two ingredients can help you get anywhere in life you want to go. It's not what you do, but why and how you do it. That's what will make any person flourish.

Let's take a look at *purpose* and *intention* in action. I remember watching a special on CNBC on the Harvard Business School. I love everything about economics, so I find it very pleasurable to view shows on CNBC. One very distinct person stood out when I was watching this special. It was a lady by the name of Kathy Giusti. She was a former graduate of the Harvard Business School.

Ms. Giusti told her story on how she was diagnosed with a very rare form of cancer called, Multiple Myeloma. She was told by doctors it was 100% fatal and she only had three years to live. At the time, she had an infant daughter and her future looked very grim. She did not succumb to depression, but instead purposed in her heart to fight this disease back! She stated in her interview that she wanted to live long enough so her daughter would remember her. She established *purpose*. Then, with *intention*, she began to formulate a plan to attack this disease. She utilized and gave great credit to Harvard Business Schools for the problem fighting skills that was executed in helping her fight.

Now 15 years later, she not only lived beyond the three years the doctors gave her, she developed and started a very prominent non-profit agency. This agency helped create many different drugs to help other people double their life expectancy. She and her organization have raised multiple millions of dollars for cancer research and have been named one of Time Magazines Most Influential People. She gave a couple of ingredients on success in one of her commencement speeches to graduates that I will share with you:

> "Setting a goal you are passionate about and building a plan."

> "Taking risks. I was not a risk taker, but when I faced my own mortality, my risk profile changed dramatically."

"Persevering, no matter how high and daunting the obstacles. I have faced chemotherapy. I ran endless meetings in scarves hiding my bald head. I endured a bone marrow transplant and isolation. I travel every week concerned about infections. Through it all, I have persevered and stayed focused on the mission."

"Pick your partners wisely. You must work with people who energize you, who share your dreams."

Armed with purpose and passion, you can create things that will help others. You can help leave a legacy for people who are coming behind you!

#LIFE'S PIT STOPS

Enjoy the journey. Let's face it...we live in a busy world! There is something always to be done especially when you have responsibilities like: children, mortgage payments, and other obligations to attend to, on a daily basis. Something is always there to take away your time, like a tiny child begging for juice. If we are not careful, we will look up one day and life would have passed us by. Sometimes, we are so busy trying to get to the destination, we forget to enjoy the journey. Some people are just trying to make it day to day, stressed out, sick, and discouraged. But, take a moment and enjoy what I call life's bite sized enjoyable moments.

For example, one day I was running late for a meeting. I was trying to find my shirt. For some reason, when it is time for me to be somewhere, my clothes magically grow arms and legs, wanting to play hide and seek! So here I am, running through the house looking for my shirt while my children are at the kitchen table having their cereal. My son always tries to emulate me and he begged for some cologne of his own. Of course, we were not going to give him some expensive cologne. He was only eight years old as the time. So, we got him some knock off spray cologne. I finally found my shirt and my son says, "Daddy, you forgot to put on your cologne." I turned around and looked for my cologne and he says, "Daddy, you can use mine!"

I gave him a nervous look praying to find my own cologne bottle. I was looking at him with a nervous smile, still trying to find my own cologne. Although, he insisted and said, "Daddy, try my cologne." My daughter, Hannah, who was seven at the time says, with a loud deep voice, "Yeah, you have cologne, but it stinks!" At that moment, I just burst into laughter. She started to laugh along with my other children. At that moment, time did not matter. I was just enjoying the moment that God allowed me to experience. However, if I had not paid attention to it, I would have been upset that I was running late for my meeting. I would have been mad at my wife for not tying my shirt down so it would not walk away. That situation could have gone in a totally different direction.

I want you to realize that it is important sometimes to stop and just close your eyes, and just think quietly. Remember when you had a good time with a friend, a coworker, or your children. It may have been something you did for someone else or it may have been something joyful you experienced. Take a deep breath and enjoy those moments! One thing that will happen is that your brain will recognize those moments in the future. You will begin to take notice and begin to enjoy those moments. By doing this, you will bring a greater level of joy in your life and will help add years to your life.

Stress is a killer and it is designed to break you! Stress is designed to wear you completely out. Over time, it brings sickness to the body and create other diseases. The bible tells us in Proverbs 17:22 that, *"A cheerful heart does good like a medicine, but a dry spirit dries up the bones."* If you are dealing with sickness in your body, or any other stress or concern, find some good people to hang out with or a good funny movie, and just be determined that you are going to enjoy the moment. Say to yourself, "I am going to laugh the loudest, even until tears come down my face." If you implement this, watch the changes that will be introduced into your life.

One day, earlier this year, I was riding in my car. This was right around graduation season. I saw a very nice current year Cadillac pull up beside me. I had to take a double look because what I discovered it was completely covered in Graffiti. It read the current class year and other weird names. It seemed like something out of a movie or something. It was completely covered. I thought to myself the owners of that vehicle must be really relaxed because I know the average person would not allow that! Then, I thought how much I used to be like those kids, wild, crazy and spontaneous, with not a care in the world, just enjoying life.

I then realized, when we get older, we slowly lose that energy and happiness. We lose that spontaneity because reality hits us and we become the majority of people out there. I understand we should mature to a certain extent.

So, I am not saying we should always live like a high school teenager. However, if we can extract the good portion from our youth to maintain some of that carefree living attitude, that would be good.

If we dare to believe that there is nothing in this world we cannot handle, at that moment, you will begin to live life with a different mindset. If you choose to view life from a different mindset, you will make different choices. Make a choice to decide that you are worth living! Change is only a mind change away.

I remember when Pharrell introduced the world to his hit song, "Happy." It exploded phenomenally on an international scale. He achieved what rarely artists can achieve, and that's having us all singing the same song! I also remember this particular clip of "Happy" on YouTube. It had people from all over the world and from all walks of life: African Americans, Caucasians, Hispanics, Chinese, French and all types of diversity of people singing the same song. It was such an inspirational video. If you were not touched by watching this video then I advise you to go to the doctors, because your cry meter is broke. Watching this video and knowing that no matter the race, gender or social status, that deep down inside, people just want happiness out of this thing we call life.

The worlds view sometimes give many definitions to happiness. They say money will bring happiness, but we scratch our heads when celebrities take their own life! We recently lost a great comedic, icon Robin Williams. Many debated on his net worth to the tune of 100's of millions. But, we can guess with a high probability, that he was not penniless when he took his own life. Others say relationships brings happiness, thinking, "If I were only married, then I would be happy."

We see the divorce rate steadily climbing. When people say "I do," they really don't realize to what extent they're saying "I do" to. When the butterflies of excitement wear off and the guests go home, they have to now live with this same person day in and day out. There's no more wedding planning, setting appointments, and cake tasting. There's no more being filled with the excitement of how you going to look in that dress. Furthermore, from the guys' aspect, how glad you will be when you won't have to write another check for things you agreed to purchase. People say "I do" so haphazardly, not even realizing what they said! When she came to you, you just shook your head and said, "Ok. Yep and ok Honey!" You start on a journey with the supposed person of your dreams. Then, it becomes not so exciting anymore. What you thought made you happy and what you built your expectations on is slowly leaving you! Lastly, you feel like if this were significant, you would feel happy about it.

You take on projects that's above your head as you try to outshine everyone else. You never say no to anything. At the end of the day, you still feel empty and alone. However, you feel that you carry a level of significance. When you come around, they say, "Give it to (insert your name here). He can get it done. He never complains and he does good work." When everyone else is satisfied with your work, you decide to pat yourself on the back. Nevertheless, you still feel empty. You thought being important and significant would bring you happiness! True happiness is having trust and confidence in a higher power that's beyond your natural ability to see.

#HAPPINESS IS NOT A FEELING – IT'S A DECISION

Happiness comes from trust! Let me explain it to you this way. My wife and I had a situation at our local bank. Money had been deducted from our account without our permission. We were victims of bank fraud. In the beginning of this situation, there were huge amounts of money being debited as there were pending checks that we had written to take care of household bills among other things. I said "Oh Lord, those checks will be bouncing from here (Michigan) to California!" I was stressing out. I contacted my bank and after hours of talks with my bank representatives, taking documents in and filling out forms, they told us, "Mr. and Mrs. Hartwell, we see your accounts were used fraudulently. We are not only putting your money back into your account, but when any checks you've written come in, we are guaranteeing we will pay them. No checks will be rejected!" Immediately, a feeling of peace and joy came over my body! At that moment, my account had not changed not one bit, because the banker said it would take a couple days to get things straight. But, because of the bankers word, I was immediately at peace and happy with the outcome of this situation.

So have happiness and peace knowing that God did not put you on this earth to fail. He does not make defective products, but he puts his best foot forward to make you! You are God's prized POSSESSION. Have happiness in knowing that nothing you're going through or whatever you're trying to do, God is with you. Whatever your situation is, He will get you through it!

#HOT TOPIC

You know we live in a world where our culture is ever changing and things that are popular today will not be popular tomorrow. Literally, our culture is ever evolving! One thing that will not change is gossip! I rarely have any down time but when I do, I catch episodes of The Wendy Williams show. She has a segment in her show which is called "Hot Topics." It's a segment where she discusses the latest celebrity news. I sat there and watched. I was rather entertained. I must admit, I don't gossip about people. However, I was very entertained by what Wendy was saying in regards to the latest celebrity gossip. I began forming my own opinions about certain situations on which Mrs. Williams was speaking on.

Then, I suddenly realized that people will be entertained by your success or failures and not even live their own! Look at all these rappers who give an image of success, riches, and fame. Look at how young people, and some old, try to emulate these people. They are not being who they are, but trying to live through someone else. Then you have people who tried to succeed and maybe they failed. We form opinions about what they did wrong, when the people who judging have not done anything! If they tried and failed, then guess what, at least they tried! Don't ever be distracted of what others may think or feel about you! People change and so does their opinion about you.

#EMOTIONS - HAVE THEM! DON'T LET THEM HAVE YOU

I have always been intrigued by personal success and personal growth. I'm a big fan of different types of motivational speakers, and the principles that they speak upon. I stumbled upon a book by Brian Tracy entitled, "Discipline." He stated something in this book that really stuck with me. He stated, "Successful people utilize discipline to achieve great things. They have feelings of not wanting to be like everyone else, but they use self-discipline to override how they feel to achieve greatness." I began to think about how so many of us are being controlled by our emotions. So much so, that they have us held captive and will not allow us to excel beyond our potential!

I remember one day having some flimsy emotions! I was having a very rough day. The moment I put on my headphones and began listening to music, my mood changed almost immediately! Before listening, I was tired and not feeling well. I wanted to just lay down and shut my eyes. I had a lot of things on my "To Do" list and the more I sat, the more things got added to this list. However, the moment I heard my favorite songs, that all changed! I posed this question to myself, "How is it that some of us can base our lives on some negative emotion, but that situation can be changed by a simple song?"

Some of us make decisions in the moment of emotional frustration that can take years to get over or to fix. We must realize, some things just cannot be fixed! You can always tell emotionally controlled people. They're really not hard to notice. They are usually the ones getting upset and making a scene at restaurants, grocery stores or some other public place. However, this is my favorite, those people who type hate filled messages on Facebook for the world to see! They have no discretion. Their lives are usually filled with missed opportunities and regrets! These are people who have fully given their life to emotions.

Emotions are not bad, don't get me wrong. Examples of positive emotions would be the following: when you see your first child born, you get the job you've always wanted, you finally graduate or accomplish something that you always wanted to accomplish. When you accomplish these things, you cannot help, but to feel good! God gave us emotions to enjoy and experience life, not for our emotions to control us. No matter what goes on in your life, you cannot be swayed by your emotions.

People who are fulfilled have these traits in common. My grandfather worked for General Motors for more than forty years. He and my grandmother were brought up with strict working habits. My Grandmother, nor my grandfather, had the opportunity to attend school like other nationalities of children did. Since they were born and raised in Mississippi, they had to work in cotton fields with their parents. One thing their parents instilled in them was discipline! They would get up early in the morning and work until sundown, seven days a week. They worked hard, only to get cheated in wages by a wholesaler, because my great-grandfather could not count well. They eventually migrated to up north to Michigan. No matter how they felt, they still worked as if they still on the cotton field.

My grandfather worked at General Motors, without rarely missing a day. My grandmother ran a non-profit organization, helping to feed and clothe the homeless. She fed and clothed thousands in the Flint, Michigan area. Even today, people all over the city call her "Mother." My Grandparents accumulated numerous of real estate properties. They purchased, owned and managed several rental properties that they still have. They achieved so much with very little education. I remember and glean so much from them. One thing my Grandmother told me is, "I don't care how you feel, you must work!" I have not always exemplified that trait when I was younger, but the older I got, I realize how important it was! She never let me miss a day in school because "feelings" did not matter! When you learn to put emotions aside and not be led by them, you can achieve great things!

#Have a Plan –
DEVELOPING STRATEGIES TO WIN

One night, my wife and I were asleep in our bed. We were in the stage of training our two oldest children, Matthew and Hannah, how to sleep in their own rooms. They couldn't have been no more than ages four and five, respectfully. We would lay them in their beds every night. In the morning, we would wake up and there the both of them would be in our beds - one under my armpit and the other one with her leg halfway around my wife's neck. I would be very upset. The twins were just born, so we had two cribs to watch at night in our room. Our two oldest made it very difficult for us to get our rest.

One night I thought to myself, "I will fix them! I am going to lock my door!" I put them in the bed, and had a sense of joy within myself, because I am thinking, "I got them this time! I am going to enjoy my sleep without kids in my bed!" I closed the door and locked it as tight as it would go and scurried off to bed. To my amazement, I woke up and there were the kid snuggled right in the same spot as before. Being slightly upset and utterly confused, I waited until they woke up and asked them, "How did you get in my room?" My son looks at me with a nervous look and said, "Well, when Hannah and I could not open your door, I took a barrette out of Hannah's hair, put it in the door knob and twisted it. It let us in!" I looked bewildered and perplexed as to how that idea came to a little five year olds brain? He was determined to get inside my door, because they were afraid to stay in their own room! He had a strategic way on how he was going to accomplish his goal. He was not going to allow any obstacle to get in his way!

We can abstract certain pearls of wisdom from this story! We must first have the mindset of winning! If you have not won in your mind, it will never happen in reality. If you cannot see it, it will never happen. Everything you see, such as a beautiful building, an airplane, or a car, it was first seen in someone's mind! They had enough faith to compel them to action to make it happen, and bring it into the physical manifestation! How crazy is it for the Wright Brother's to make an object that would fly humans in the air? That's not common! They were not competing with another company to build airplanes. But, it came from an idea that they worked and worked, then perfected!

In the beginning, when God created the heavens and the earth, it was a glorious time! When God created man, he gave Adam a job. One of his jobs was to name the animals. Now, there was no instruction manual or any training prior to Adam accepting this job! So my question is, what in him came to the realization that he could just look at an elephant and say, "I will call you Elephant or any other animal, for that matter?" How could he do something like that?

How could there be no reference on how to do something that was never done before? Because, God made us in His image. We have been equipped with everything we need to succeed. Quit looking around, blaming failure on other things and people. I want you to believe in yourself! Know that God has equipped you with everything you need to succeed.

How do we develop winning strategies? First of all, we have to understand why we have to be strategic in life if we want to be prosperous! Anything you want to accomplish has to takes steps, or strategies, to arrive at your goal! Maybe you or a loved one needed to have surgery. When you arrive at the hospital, and before the surgeon wheels you or your loved one to the operating room, many times the surgeon will have a consultation with you to explain their experience. What if they tell you they just woke up one morning and decided to become a surgeon? Then, as they begin to explain with the look of an excited surgeon, they inform you that they never went to school. They learned just by watching many surgical tapes. They go on to say, that they have never missed an episode of "Grey's Anatomy" and "ER" and sometimes would watch reruns of M.A.S.H. on the weekends! I can guarantee you that within seconds, you would be out of that bed, running to the nearest exit to call the police.

My point in this example is that surgeons had to take a certain level of educational requirement and maintain a certain grade average to obtain the authority to perform surgery on people. He had to purpose in his mind what he wanted to be and then have a road map to get to his goal.

In this next section, I would like to share some steps with you that has helped me out in my life. Even though these steps are not a cure for all, I am sure that you can extract from them and use them in your life.

Step 1
Write down some goals of what you want to accomplish. These rules are not set in stone, but it will give you a road map to where you are going. It will make it clear and you'll have a workable blueprint to use. You would be surprised by what ideas pop into your head on specific ways you can obtain your goals.

Step 2
Identify your partners. Dr. I. V. Hillard, pastor of New Light Church in Houston, Texas, once quoted, "Success was never meant to be a solo flight". My wife and I have particular indulgences, one of which is we love to go to the movies. With our busy schedules, from raising a family to running our businesses and serving people, we allow ourselves two treats a week, which are going to dinner and the movies. Well, we've noticed that at the end of every movie, people never stay long enough to watch the credits. One day, I was watching Captain America 2. I know if you're watching a Marvel

movie, you have to stay until the end to catch sneak peeks of upcoming movies! As I was sitting there, I began to look at all the names of people who helped this movie come to life. One thing I understood is that without these people, companies and talents, this movie would have not been possible. Then it hit me. In order to be a successful, you must first be humble enough to understand you need help. The level of success you want to achieve is determined by the network of people with whom you surround yourself. When Jesus came on the scene He started recruiting disciples, which, in essence, were His partners.

It was stated by former partners of Steve Jobs, the founder and CEO of one of the most successful companies in the world, that he never wrote one single code. He did, however, surrounded himself with people who knew how to code. Saying this, you must identify your partners. Show people your plan. Don't be afraid of rejection! Everyone in this world will not tell you no! Your 'yes' is out there. You just have to believe it.

You can connect with your local Chamber of Commerce or try to attend networking events. Visit websites like Meetup.com, where they have functions designed to meet new people. Commit to introducing yourself to one new person a week. If that's too much, try to introduce yourself to, at least, one person a month. By the end of the year, you would have met twelve new people.

Set reminder alerts on your Smartphone to remind yourself to introduce yourself to different people. Make sure to set it when you know you will be out of the house, like right after work when you usually stop and get gas or buy groceries. This will make it easier to introduce yourself. You would be surprised how effective this is, because you never know with whom you would be shaking hands with. You could start a general conversation by complimenting what they're wearing or stating something about a current event. This is a small step, but can be so effective.

Step 3

This step is the most crucial part. It is the glue that will help bring anything you want into your life. That is DISCIPLINE! Many people don't like this word and even run from it. However, some of the most successful people have this one trait in common. Discipline is often mislabeled as something bad. But, it is something great, if you master it. You can accomplish things you would never have thought that were possible. Famous motivational speaker, Jim Rohn, was quoted as saying, "Discipline is the bridge between goals and accomplishment."

What is *self-discipline*? Self- discipline is enforcing your body and mind to come into alignment with what you want to accomplish. Discipline is something that must be developed. You cannot think that one day you will wake up and be totally disciplined. You will not wake up eating all of the right foods, you will not wake up exercising twenty hours a day, nor will wake up saying all of the right things every time. It takes small acts of *self-discipline* that will begin to shape who you are. People get discouraged because they do not see change right away. They neglect one component that will add to the small steps. That one component is momentum! Once you begin to take small steps, it will take time. Once you start to believe you can, it will become an addictive habit!

I was once watching this weight loss show. At the beginning of this show, this guy started out weighing over 500 lbs. I began to feel sorry for this guy, because every exercise this guy did was like he was in complete agony. Every step he made, he was absolutely uncomfortable. But, slowly it was like a light bulb went on in this guys' head. He began to push harder. He began to believe that he could do it! A couple weeks later, he had set a record while running on the treadmill. He, of course, shedded the weight quicker than anyone I have ever seen! I know it was TV. Normally, they update the viewer on the timeframe of each contestant, what took him years to gain, he lost within a couple of months. You may think that it takes too long to master *self- discipline*, but once momentum kicks in, time will accelerate every day. Start making small steps and document them. See where you are at the end of the week. It seems small, but those small, seemingly insignificant steps, will soon become great strides towards your goals.

When I was a little boy, we use to love to race against each other. I remember playing with my cousins and it being a hot summer day and we would all line up together taking our runner stances. We would have to have already picked a place where we were running to. We were all so determined to be the winner, we'd anxiously just be waiting on the leader to yell, "Ready? Set! GO!" One vivid memory was, I thought I was going to win this particular race, but I ended up tripping on a small rock and took a total wipe out and skinned my knee. Along with that, I bruised my ego!

Like many of us, we never come into this life to fail. We all train for the "big race" and get into our runner stance. At that moment, we think we have everything we need in life. Then "life" yells, "Ready? Set! GO!" We, then, encounter rocky bumps along the way. When we take wipe outs and bruise our egos, we must not only anticipate them, but, when they happen, we must become flexible! Being flexible allows us to become less frustrated when things happen or when things don't happen according to our plan. Especially when you have the personality of a person who plans out everything by having every "I" dotted and every "T" crossed. This personality type is what I call a perfectionist.

Other personalities that are not as caught up in details will not be as frustrated. They will give up on the goal altogether. When things get hard, they quit. This cycle repeats often and rarely are they ever able to finish anything. No matter what your personality type is, you have to learn to become flexible. A mind of a flexible person is always thinking of an alternative ending to every personal goal. Just because door "A" is closed, they always want to know what's behind door "B". They never quit on their journey to obtain the goal. People who quickly give up in frustration can be compared to a crying baby who does not get their way. Those are the types of people who will never obtain their goals and will often be invited to celebrate others in their achievements.

The statement I just made may seem tough, but I see this cycle repeated within too many people. I simply do not want you to make the same mistake. Successful people are not successful because they do everything perfect. They are not successful because they are the smartest person who execute the cutting edge strategy. They are mainly successful because they did not give up when things went against them.

When Walt Disney embarked upon opening the Disney World Park, nothing worked! He had to postpone the opening and had to disappoint a lot of people. He may have seemed like failure, but he did not give up! He became flexible and realized that there were many things that he could not control. One thing that contributed to this was the weather. There was a significant amount of moisture in the air which caused much of the rides' technology to fail and not work properly. This was something he could not predict. He did not give up or whine about it. He was able to remain flexible. Because of his never give up disposition, we are able to enjoy many things that are produced and created by the Disney Corporation.

#BE SPECIFIC – POWER OF CLARITY

I recently started wearing glasses a couple of years ago. I did not grow up wearing glasses, like my wife. She is pretty accustomed to wearing glasses. For me, it took a minute to get used to them. I often left them everywhere I went and would have to return to get them. My wife would always catch me squinting and trying hard to focus on things I was trying to read. I remember taking the big plunge and switched to contact lenses, thinking it would be better scenario for me. When I got my glasses, as well as when I got my contact lenses, the doctor told me, "Mr. Hartwell, I know things may seem a little blurry at first, but keep your glasses on and your eyes will get adjusted." I remember how challenging it was in the beginning. However, things were so clear! I did not have to squint. I didn't have to put things directly up to my eyes to read. It was such a relief. Now, I cannot even function without my glasses! I wake up and don't take one step without putting them on, because my eyesight is so much clearer with them! When I don't wear my glasses, I am not completely blind! I can make out objects. If I try hard enough and read something close enough, I can actually read a book!

In your life, you may can function with having a vague future. It's not until you get clarity, can you see the full picture of where you're headed. Clarity is such a key ingredient. Whenever you see an athlete compete, they do not face their opponent without visualizing with clarity. They visualize obtaining the victory and they a clear picture of them winning in their category.

Many times people know what they want, however, they forget the crucial part of attending to the details. There is an old saying, "The devil is in the details!" I heard someone say something so significant, that it bears repeating! When there is clarity of vision, it accelerates the goal! Have you ever got lost driving somewhere? Maybe it was foggy out or snowing. You were just plain lost! You were driving at a slow pace, trying to look at street names, building numbers, or nearby business. While you are trying to find your destination, you are slowing down and your trip is getting prolonged. Now, compare that to a person who actually knows their destination. They can enjoy the scenery and are so confident. They can take alternative routes to get to their destination. When you have lack of clarity, your trip to success will continue to get delayed. Much like the driver who lacks clarity, they get frustrated and ultimately get tired and turn around.

Many people have given up and turned around. I have a good feeling, however, that those who are reading this book have a good chance of not turning back and accelerating towards their goals in life. You can start by writing those plans down and getting as detailed as possible about them. Write down dates and journal the feelings that you will experience in achieving your goals. For example, "I will complete my book by November 20, 2014. I will have a feeling of joy, knowing that I will touch someone's life and they will feel help in their time of need." That is a simple task to complete.

Let's even take it a step further. The bible states in Habakkuk 2:2, "And the LORD answered me: "Write the vision; make it plain on tablets, so he may run who reads it." We can easily replace the word "plain" with make it "clear." I would hope that you can extract from this simple principle and apply it to your master plan of success!

#POWER OF FOCUS

If you will have an open heart, you can hear something that will help enhance and enrich your life. Six years ago, my wife began to have stomach cramps. We had suspected she may have been pregnant. So, when we went to the hospital, they confirmed our suspicions. The nurse held a device up to my wife's stomach and leaned into her device monitor. She slightly grunted the word "Hum!" I did not think anything of it. I was just concerned about my wife! She then leaned back in her chair and grunted the same word, "Hummm!" My wife and I were concerned after two "Hums!"

The nurse then said to us, "Mr. and Mrs. Hartwell, I am hearing two heart beats!" She then turned the monitors up and allowed us to hear those heart beats! We were absolutely stunned. I was also terrified! Throughout the pregnancy, she had many complications, more than we anticipated. I remember, by a couple of months in, I was utterly exhausted! I remember thinking, "Okay, six more months to go!" Then, I thought, "I cannot do this!" What was supposed to be a happy time, became a time of anxiety and stress for me, because I allowed it to be. You see, I was focused on the journey and not the end result. I was allowing anxiety and fear to grip my heart.

Anxiety is the same thing as being impatient. Many of us get off track and allow our dreams to go unlived, because we focus on the journey, instead of the end result. When we focus on the journey, we tend to think we want it right now. Sometimes, we think we have to give up certain things. For example, if we want to lose weight, we immediately feel pain. We experience this pain because we focus on the fact that we have to give up those ice cream binges we are so use to doing every night before bed.

If we aspire to complete a life goal by going into a profession that requires a degree, we immediately think about the years of schooling it would take. Instead of thinking of the negative aspects of wanting to lose weight, we think how healthy we would be. You can focus on how you can live longer and enjoy your spouse and your children. You can have more energy! You will feel better and come off the medication the doctors have you on. In obtaining that degree, instead of thinking how long it would take, think about how your family would be proud of you. Think about the doors of opportunity that a degree can open up for you.

Whatever we tend to focus on is what we can accomplish. What happens if we tend to focus on the wrong things? For an example, I was on a very popular social media site and someone posted a photo of a very expensive luxury mansion. The home was very big and sat on a lake. Many people commented on the photo.

To my surprise, many comments were highly negative. People were posting comments like, "Wow! That's a big house. It would take a lot to clean something like that!" Another person said, "That's a huge house! Who would need all that space? That's just too much house! Wow, it would take me a week to clean that big house! I bet you its haunted!" The picture was meant to be something beautiful, but people were focused on the wrong things. Their minds immediately went to what was wrong, instead of what was right. I thought to myself, "If you could afford a home like that, you could afford a cleaning staff to clean it!" In response about this house being too much for a person, who says it's just one person living in the home? When we become so focused on the journey to our destination, the more our minds will make up excuses not take actions to complete the goal.

As my wife carried our twins, I would have taunting fears that would torment me throughout the day. I would envision myself sitting in the doctors' office and the doctor telling me they do not hear a heartbeat anymore and my wife lost the babies! I love my children too much and I felt like I could not take something happening to my children.

One day, my wife was having stomach cramps and bleeding, I remember driving her to the hospital thinking, "This is it!" I was trying to keep the faith, but that little voice of doubt was inside saying, "This is it! They're about to tell me they don't hear a heartbeat." When we arrived at the hospital, she checked in to be examined by the doctor. While she was in examining room, I can remember a still small voice came to me and said, "Everything is going to be ok. Stop worrying about it!" A calmness came over me. I had a friend to pray with me and he spoke words of comfort to me. The doctors came out and said, "Everything is okay! The reason for the bleeding was because the babies are growing. It's common in pregnancy, especially with twins, because they are taking up more space!" I left that hospital relieved! My wife knew I was worried. She would often times distract me with picking baby names or planning out their room. She would also suggest we shop for the little ones. She was helping me refocus my thought process, so that my mind would not go straight to worrying. It would go to a happy place.

I don't want you focusing on the journey. I want you to imagine the end result. Retrain how you think. Once you do that, you will find it easier to accomplish your goals. When you write down your road map, begin to think about what it will feel like when it's completed. Allow your mind to make it come alive. As you do this continually, you will find that the task will become easy. You will find yourself producing things at such a momentum. Don't allow yourself to be distracted by the journey, but focus on the end goal. In your journey, I want to bring your attention to this scripture found in Colossians 3:2, *"Set your minds on things that are above, not on things that are on earth."* I want you to extract this nugget of comfort from this passage. You have the ability to actually set your own mind. Saying this, I want you to set your mind on the end results. In that, you will find yourself getting things accomplished like you never have before. This book is a product of myself focusing on my goals, and accomplishing them.

#DISTRACTIONS! HOW TO MANAGE THEM

Distractions - We all have them. They disguise themselves as many things. Have you ever sat down at your computer and was determined to get some work done, only to look up hours later and you have not completed anything? I have many times gotten fed up with delaying things I know I needed to get done. I get all pumped up and determined because I am going to get that report done. I say to myself, "I am going to add to my next book, script or business plan... Today is the day!" I sit down and open my Google Drive account to whichever project I am working on. I open it up and say, "Well, let me just take a look at my Facebook news feed real quick. Hmmm, what's this? Taylor Swift yanks all her music from streaming websites? The president of Spotify responds to Taylor Swift?" Before I know it, I have clicked the link to read it. By now, the little stories at the bottom have caught my attention also. So, I end up checking statuses on Facebook. I end up finishing the night off on Youtube. By this time, I'm tired. I look at the time and it's time for bed.

I've haven't even touched any of my projects! Sounds familiar?

We live in a world that never sleeps! Current events are always happening and the ever evolving technology is ever evolving. Social media, TV networks, and publications are all competing for your attention. They spend multi-billions of marketing dollars a year to pique your interest, so that you can become a continuous viewer. Distractions! Besides the myriad of corporations, you have people in your life that desires your time. Whether it's the rambunctious children, your nagging spouse, your relentless teachers, your bossy bosses, or your "loving" parents and siblings, it doesn't matter. They are all lined up around the block, as if Oprah were giving away her "favorite things," wanting your attention.

A few years ago, my wife and I purchased a trampoline for our children. They were so excited! They began to bounce around and scream. With all five little faces smiling and laughing in sheer fun. As they were jumping around doing flips, we were watching for a few minutes, just to see their enjoyment. We grew tired of it after a couple of minutes, then tried to get into the house to get some work done. Out of nowhere, we heard screams, 'Daddy! Mommy! Look at me! Watch this!" My son did a backflip. We cheered for him like we were on a football field, rooting for our home team. Once again, we attempted to go into the house, to no avail. We begin to hear even more screams from all the kids, "Look at me! Look at me!" Even our youngest daughter, who was one year old at the time, was trying to formulate syllables to say, 'Look at me, Mommy and Daddy!" Although it came out as gibberish, her body contortions were such as we knew what she was trying to say.

We only intended to watch for a few minutes. However, we ended up spending the majority of the day with them outside in the back yard. Things will compete to distract you, but you always have to remember one thing - you are in control of your time!

The main reason a person loses focus quickly is a lack of discipline. When you don't have discipline in an area, you don't have any protection from any distracting thoughts or impulses that come your way. This will ultimately lead to frustrations. Things begin to pile up. If you're in a relationship, the quality of your relationship begins to be demolished because of this lack of focus. Just know, as I was typing these sentences, my phone began to send me alerts. Someone was sending me messages through a messenger application I have. The conversation started out encouraging. Then, it took a turn into a sales pitch, for which I did not have time. Since I had begun working on myself in this area, I immediately responded that I was not available now and asked if we could schedule an appointment later that week. I ended up cutting the conversation short and booked an appointment later that week to discuss the offer, when I had time.

You see, when you have self-control or discipline, you can easily take back control of your valued time, and not allow yourself to be side tracked by things that can wait. From that experience, I decided, by moving forward, I would not have my phone on during my writing sessions. It's called "Limiting Your Distractions." Discipline is like having your own private bouncer. They screen all the thoughts that try to crash your life. Once they come knocking, easily they are rejected from your mind. You can keep moving to complete the task until it is finished. A good tip for helping with discipline is meditation. It has always helped me get a clearer perspective. I meditate on my goals. I would imagine how I would feel if they were completed. This has tremendously helped me stay focused and helped to keep my eyes on the end goal.

Our smart phones have quickly become one of the greatest sources of distraction in our lives. The average person now checks their mobile phone more than 150 times a day, just short of every six waking minutes. To limit the distracting nature of your smart phone, turn off all nonessential notifications, such as email, Facebook, Twitter, games, etc. as a default setting. As a result, you will be able to check your apps on your schedule, and at appropriate times throughout the day.

Our lives and minds are often cluttered and distracted by the many unfinished projects around us, such as unanswered emails, household chores, or financial responsibilities. Fortunately, many of these projects can be completed in far less time than we think. To live with less distraction, if a project can be completed in less than two minutes, adopt a "One-Minute Rule" mentality.

Just like physical clutter distracts our attention, digital clutter accomplishes the same. Desktop icons, opened programs, and other visible notifications jockey for unannounced attention in our mind. Notice the digital triggers that grab your attention. Make a mental note to ruthlessly remove them.

One of the most helpful and practical pieces of advice I ever received about keeping focused, is the simple solution of keeping a to-do list handy and current. No matter how hard you try to manage yourself, new responsibilities and opportunities will surface in your mind from internal and external sources. The opportunity to quickly write down the task allows it to be quickly discarded from your mind. I use this as a simple, easy-to-use opportunity list.

The value of your life is not measured by the number of "likes" your Facebook post receives or the number of positive comments on your blog post. Please understand, there is great value in humbly seeking opinion and appreciating the wise counsel of those who love you. But, there is no value in wasting mental energy over the negative criticism of those who only value their own self-interests. Learn to recognize the difference. Let's stop living distracted over the opinions of people who don't matter.

There is little doubt our world is filled with constant distraction—it always has been. Furthermore, there is little doubt that those who achieve the greatest significance in life learn to manage them effectively—they always have.

I had an experience on a warm summer day back in 1997. I remember the day never felt so right. I was seventeen at the time and my cousin, Tanika, and I found out that our favorite musical artist was coming to Michigan. There were roughly four to five five performers coming, but my cousin was interested in seeing Ginuwine. However, I had an obsession with Aaliyah. Our teenage years were like any other misguided teen who was fascinated by a person's stage persona. I remember purchasing the ticket from my neighborhood music store called, Music Planet. "One ticket please!" I said with a loud, anxious voice. By the looks of the salesman eyes, I knew that he knew that day I was not playing. I wanted good seats no matter what the price was. The day could not have been any better. I made up in my mind that I was going to meet this young lady I thought I loved. I wanted her to know how much I loved her. Now that I look back at this moment, it seems silly and even disturbing! But, I had the assurance no way we were going to be in the same building and were not going to meet! As my cousin pulled up to the stadium, it was almost like I had the blueprints of the Palace of Auburn Hills downloaded in my mind! I looked at all exits and noticed that one of the exits had all of the tour busses. At the other exit, there were limousines. I knew the artists were not on busses. So, it was a high probability that Aaliyah would be in a limo. I marked my exit to remember after the concert. When we got into the building, we enjoyed a couple of other artists, then Aaliyah gave a glorious performance, as the place was filled with anticipation. She belted out notes from her multi-platinum selling album as they lowered her from the ceiling. In that moment, it was almost like an angelic being came to visit earth. As she sang, we sang along with her as true fans would. When she got done, she left by the back stage exit and there was my chance.

I got up from my seat and left as if an alarm had went off at the Palace of Auburn Hills. There was one more act to perform. However, my cousin barely noticed that I was gone because I had left so fast. I walked through the halls at a pace of a person whose bladder was full and was about to explode. My walk was swift, but not too fast, because I did not want to tip off the security people and make myself look suspicious. "Oh great, an elevator!" I thought to myself, "Here is my chance to get to the door quicker!" I waited patiently for the elevator to open up. It seemed like forever! I can just picture myself meeting her and it was finally here. I could hardly wait! The door opened and my dreams were dashed as a slightly overweight police officer was sitting in a chair on the elevator reading a newspaper, kindly awaiting people of my kind! "Crap!!!!" I screamed. He looked at me and had a slight grin on his face. It was almost like his look said, "You tried it!"

As the door closed, he went back to reading his paper to await the next crazed fan! I thought to myself it has to be another way! I ran to the other side as I remembered the exit where she was coming out. I saw the door. It was blocked with a security officer. I shouted, "This can't be!" Only one person was blocking me from achieving my dream. I was not accepting this! This seeming defeat, called for drastic measures. I took my hand and put it on my throat to communicate that I couldn't breathe. I took my other hand, put it on my chest and I belted out with a loud voice, "I am having a asthma attack. I can't breathe!" The look on the security officer's face was one of definite concern. He rushed over and nervously asked, "Are you okay?" I said, "No! I need my inhaler. It's in the car and I need to get out of this door to get my inhaler! If cameras had been on me, I have no doubt in my mind, I could have earned an Oscar, or, at least, a nomination. I never had asthma or an inhaler, but all I had was determination.

He looked at me and said, "Okay Sir. I will allow you out this door." I limped my way through the door and he looked concerned and very helpful. I walked out the door and ran to the private entrance. Aaliyah's limo had just pulled up. Her dancers walked out first. Then, low and behold, she walked out in a leather jacket with matching leather pants and a leather hat! Her hair was so luxuriously long and flowing like in all her music videos. She smiled at me and I ran to her like any crazy fan would and blurted out,

"I love you!" I took her hand, and kissed it. She saw that it was an innocent gesture and was polite and courteous. She got into her limo and drove off! As I look back on all these memories, I am no different than teenagers are today. Well, maybe not as extreme as today's youth. When I see the fans react to performances by of groups such as, One Direction and artists like Taylor Swift, it's like night and day.

You may be asking, "What does this have to with me?" When you truly set your heart and focus on a goal, you will accomplish it! You may come up with many plans and strategies, but please understand that some of them may not work out. I can guarantee it. You, however, can never stop trying. Strategies or plans are not a guaranteed victory. It is one of many methods to obtain a single goal. If a strategy you're using fails, then try another one. Strategies are simply defined as coming up with a method that will give you a high probable chance of obtaining the goal.

Before I left Aaliyah's concert, I was determined that I was going to meet her. When all doors were blocked, I came up with a new plan. Determination is strategic key in completing your goals. Strategies are developed from a person mindset and their perspective, which is their outlook on how they would view a situation. In my quest to remain current in my quest for success, I can came up with an idea. My wife can look at the same thing and add something to my idea that would enhance it. This happens because it's coming from a different point of view.

When you feel like you have run out of plans, the next step is to borrow someone else's perspective. You may be able to extract certain things from them and add it to your strategy to accomplish your goal. God has given you so much potential. Even though the odds are stacked up against you, never look at it through your natural eyes. Look at it through the eyes of faith. Faith says "I can," but your natural eyes may say "I cannot, because of excuse one, two, three, four, or five.

I would like to share my favorite scripture with you. I specifically read this scripture in the time of uncertainty and when I am approaching a big project. It's found in 2 Corinthians 5:7, *"For we walk by Faith, not by sight."*

I pray that you will not stop, but remain focused. Go back to the drawing board and draft new plans. This time plan to win! Plan with a winning mindset, which is a mindset that says I am going to win. The strategies may change, but allow your mindset to stay the same.

#HANGING WITH THE RIGHT CROWD

My children are everything to me. Is my life busy? Yes! Is my life hectic, at times? Yup! Is it easy raising children? Definitely not! Is my life fulfilled? I would have to say an absolute Yes! However, I wish they came with an instruction manual. They are busy people with their own ideas and mindsets. But, if I watch them closely, I learn more from them than they ever will learn from myself!

Surrounding yourself with other people who are better than you, smarter than you, and have way more money than you, will change your life. My beautiful wife, L'Oreal, and I have five children, ages nine years old all the way down to two years old. My youngest daughter, Zoe, is the one I get a kick out of the most. I guess because she is the baby. My older children live normal lives and do normal kid things. Zoe, on the other hand, always seems to think she is their exact age. When we have dinner, she does not want to sit in a booster seat. She wants to sit in regular chairs, like the older kids. When it's lunch time, she does not want half a sandwich. She wants a whole one like the other kids. She never lets her size become an issue, because she has taken on the mindset, if they can do it, so can I.

You have to surround yourself with people who have more than you. You have to surround yourself with people who are more knowledgeable than you are. You have to do this if you ever want to cultivate that desire within yourself to become more than what you are. I got taught these principles while attending a program in my hometown called, SVAALTI. This acronym stands for Saginaw Valley African American Leadership Training Institute. This awesome community-wide program was able to connect me with people who were working to move our community in our region. It was also instrumental in helping me with surrounding myself with people who were like-minded and more established than I was. This opened up greater levels of desire in me to become more. I was exposed to more people who were doing what I wanted to do.

When desire is cultivated it, becomes a requirement. Whatever you desire, it's something you cannot live without. It becomes an addictive behavior until it is established in your life. I will give you a personal example of this. When I first started traveling, I was very frugal. I would find the cheapest flights available. Sometimes, those cheap plane tickets would have two, sometimes three, stops before I reached my destination. On one flight, I was traveling to Florida where I had several bad experiences. There were rude flights attendants, rude neighbors who snored, and I had to contend with a turbulent flight.

On my next trip, I caught a special flight that was really cheap. It was a non-stop flight. I took the flight, although, I never had taken a non-stop flight before. I boarded the plane and had a pleasant experience for the first time. As I got to my destination, I thought, "How pleasant that flight was and it was great how fast I arrived at my destination." Sometimes, on the cheap flight with stops, it would take me hours with layover to get where I was going. I made a decision that day, I would only fly non-stop flights from now on. I did not care what it cost. The pain of spending more money immediately disappeared when it was a requirement of me needing a non-stop flight.

Hanging around people who have more than you and know more than you, helps cultivate that desire. Whatever your desire is, it will become a requirement. I once heard a wise teacher, Dr. I. V. Hilliard say, "Desire properly incubated, becomes a requirement." Some people may say they don't know anyone around them with these attributes. Check around in your community, in your city, and state. I am pretty sure you will find someone that is doing some good things.

I made it a weekly ritual to watch a program called, "Bloomberg Game Changers". This program chronicles lives of successful people in their profession. I really get inspired by watching these people who are at the top of their game. Some of these incredible people are the CEO's and presidents of corporations of top name brands we trust and use in our everyday household.

My youngest daughter, Zoe, does not take into consideration her size or what we think as adults. She is not old enough to do most things for herself. In her mind, she feels that if she sees others doing something of interest, then that must mean she can do it, as well. Some of us need to develop this skill of going after something that is normally out of the box for us.

Furthermore, many people become intimidated and rather jealous of others who are taking the initiative to do more and to have more. This is a poor mentality. I have seen this in many people. They only surround themselves with people who are "yes" people. Those are the people who, no matter what, they agree with everything you say. I would hope that by surrounding yourself with people who inspire you to do better, will help cultivate and activate the belief that anything can be accomplished.

You have to begin to find yourself in other people. Now, listen closely. I did not say try to be other people. I suggested that you find yourself in other people. Whatever you are seeking to accomplish, someone else has already done it. Shocking, isn't it?

Now, listen even more closely. There may be someone who can do things better than you. Look at Michael Jackson. In the entertainment industry, before there was Michael Jackson, there was Elvis Presley. Within the World-Wide Boxing Federation, there was "Iron" Mike Tyson before there was "Money" Floyd Mayweather. In the NBA, there was Michael Jordan before there was Kobe Bryant...Go, Laker Nation! C'mon, please don't mail nasty letters to me over the last statement...Okay.

My point is, there is somebody already at the end of the process you are beginning. Look at the results of hard work and discipline. Know that the same air they breathe, you breathe also. They eat just like you, have feelings just like you, and put on their pants one leg at a time, just like you. Due to the onslaught of the media and the society we live in, they try to mystify success, like it's some type of special X-Men Mutant power or something. They have people believing that successful people have some type of special connection with some type of otherworldly power, or that they have made a deal with the devil. As if only the people who sell their souls to the devil become successful.

If I can take a theological approach, King Solomon was one the richest persons in the world during the Bible days. Theologians subscribe to the school of thought that he is the one who holds the title of the world's richest man to ever live. So, I would have to debunk the myth that successful people are "special." One of the differences between successful people and unsuccessful people is, successful people surround themselves with people who inspires and challenges them. They do not become intimidated or jealous of what others have or what they have accomplished. When you allow yourself to be surrounded and inspired by great people, you must take on a student mindset. You must become teachable. It does not mean they must walk up to you and say, "Hey, this is how you become successful." You learn by what you see them doing, and by studying what their routines that they follow every day. My youngest daughter, Zoe, learned a lot of what she does by what she sees my older children doing.

I would hope that you would get inspired to change your environment and to make it conducive for you to grow and excel. No one makes it to their destination without help from others. When famous people get interviewed, they always give credit to more established people that inspired them. Oprah Winfrey talks about when she first interviewed for a news anchor position. She imagined herself as a type of Barbara Walters. She gives Barbara Walters credit for inspiring her. Michael Jackson gives credit for being inspired by James Brown. Celine Dion pays homage in her sold-out Las Vegas Shows to Michael Jackson, who had a great influence on her musical career. She stated that he inspired her to learn English, as a second language, so that she could sing like him. I can go on and on, but I won't. Make a decision to surround yourself with the right crowd that you may become inspired and transformed into the person you desire to be.

#CRUTCHES & WALKERS!

I know what you are thinking...WTF?!? Crutches and walkers? What does this have to do with faith? Let me explain. My youngest sister-in-law, Chauna, is eleven years old. She would watch all the other kids riding their bikes, since she did not have one of her own. She always had to depend on waiting for her cousins to offer their bicycles to share. However, this past summer, she received a bike as a graduation present. Like any child receiving a bike, she fell in love with it. The day after her fifth grade graduation, while riding her bike, she was acting silly as any eleven year old would. Her face was filled with confidence as she embraced this new independence of a bicycle rider, which something she always loved to do. As she was riding her new bike, she experienced a very nasty fall and broke her ankle in two different places.

In the beginning, we did not realize the severity of her injury, because when she fell, a neighbor, who happened to be a nurse, witnessed the event and came to attend to Chauna. She examined her and stated she only received a sprain. This neighborly nurse informed us that she should just put ice on it and the swelling would go down.

After a few days passed, the swelling was not going down and she was still in pain. I spoke with my mother-in-law and told her I was taking her to the hospital to obtain an x-ray to see what was going on. Later that afternoon, the x-ray attendant discovered her ankle had been broken in two different places and had already begun to heal itself. However, it was incorrectly setting into place. We were totally shocked! The doctor scheduled surgery at his next availability. It took a couple months for her to get to the point of walking with the assistance of a walker, since she was rather unstable on the crutches.

The doctor stated on her last visit that her ankle is completely healed! She did not need physical therapy anymore and there was no reason for her to have any more appointments with him. But, there was a problem! She still was limping and walking with a walker. She did not feel pain or anything like that. She had just formed a new habit, a different mindset. Even though she did not feel pain anymore, she developed a new way of living that consisted of her walking with a walker when she did not even need it.

How many of us have learned how to function living beneath what we are called to be and do? Many of us have settled for less, whether it is working a dead end job or settling for bad credit with no savings. Many are settling for a person in a relationship who shows you little, to no respect. Not living up to what we dreamed to be one day, we have "walkers" and "crutches" in our lives. We have learned to live and function with them.

Now let's get to my main point that will tie this chapter together. My mother-in-law has a huge soft heart and she hates to see my little sister in any kind of discomfort or pain, so she, unlike me, allows her to walk with the walker. We've spoken about this topic many times before. She starts out being determined to put her foot down and not allow the walker. Only to find out days later, when I picked her and my sister up, Chauna comes out with her walker smiling and cheesing like a cheshire cat. Not only that, they had the nerve to decorate the walker with tennis balls at the bottom of the poles and had drawings everywhere. Imagine my disapproving expression when I saw her walking with her walker. But, deep down inside I know that my mother-in-law has a big heart, and could not resist the temptation to give into her child's desire.

I made it a point to speak with my mother-in-law again on this matter and explained to her that she does not want to enable her. I encouraged her to challenge Chauna and even take drastic measures by getting rid of the walker, all together! That would force her to re-learn how to walk without assistance. The doctor gave her a clearance and a clean bill of health.

Now, let me take a side, before I drive home my main point. We wonder why many unfortunate situations happen to us in our lives, like losing a job. Even a situation when that person we thought was the one we would marry and settle down with, finally unravels because they are not good for you. Just, maybe, that's God's way of taking the "walker" away. At that place, we will begin to discover things we never knew existed.

I remember watching a news special. At this particular time, they were highlighting some individuals who made a remarkable comeback after the financial collapse. They interviewed a young lady who opened a chain of salons and even started her very own success beauty product line. She became a very successful, very wealthy business owner. When they interviewed her, she stated she was comfortable with her job, but always wanted to start her own business. However, she did not want to leave her job. When the company that she worked for laid her off, she could not find a job because the economy was worse than it had ever been. She had no other choice but to walk and stand on her own. She got her "walker" taken away and was forced to tap into what was already in her.

As I conclude this chapter, my main point is this: you have people in your life that will challenge you. There is a difference between a good person and a right person. A good person will listen to your problem, eat with you and cry with you. The right person will listen to your problem and then give you the right advice to fix it. They may tell you things you don't want to hear. Although a right person will eat with you, they will also tell you that you cannot keep eating like this, because we need to eat more healthily. They say something like, "Let's get a salad, instead!" A right person will cry with you and then stand up and say we are not defeated! Our better days are ahead of us!

Now, I am not calling my mother-in-law a bad person. She just allowed her heart to get too involved that hampered the long-term result. Pray for the right person in your life, not just a good person. Know the difference.

#BRING IT ALL TOGETHER

I hope that after you read or listened to this book, you have started to formulate a plan of action or either plan to dust off the plan you have already created. Let it inspire you all over again! Life is a journey and the path is hardly easy and always delightful. The truth of the matter is, being successful is possible and God wants you to live your best life! Troubles never schedule their time of arrival or give you a heads up when they are coming. They are more like a cold to a child's body. They come without notice, but it leaves you stronger.

Dr. Tyeese Gaines states, that when children become ill with colds, it will build their immune system and as adults, they will have stronger immune systems. Trials can work for you, if you learn from them. There are some things that came into my life that I have sworn it will never happen again because I never want to experience that feeling again. I just want to encourage you to know that excelling is possible.

No matter if you're a person who has not lived in the best neighborhoods or you're struggling to get your business off the ground. You may be trying to maintain a company or a position within a company.

Although this book is a vehicle to guide you to success, I would not want to give an impression that you will read this, and then all of a sudden, you will begin to excel overnight. My intention is to inspire you and stir up your faith to believe in YOU! I want to awaken that potential that lives inside you. I want you to realize we are in this thing called life, together. Circumstances in life happen all the time. It doesn't matter if you've lost a business, filed for bankruptcy, was once incarcerated, or is a product of a broken home. What make successful people different from unsuccessful people is the decision they make when life happens.

Will you become depressed? Will you quit or throw in the towel? Will you continue to make excuses as to why your life is not coming together? I remember there was time in my life, I pursued a business venture. I wanted it so bad, I made some decisions and risked a lot of money in this venture. It did not work out so well. At that moment, the old me would have been depressed and would have eaten myself into a coma. But, I reflected and prayed about the situation. Then, I realized that I am responsible for my own success!

In my theological stance and in my desire to strengthen my reasoning for this conclusion, I would like to review Joshua 1:8, which states, *"Keep this Book of the Law always on your lips; meditate on it day and night, so that you may be careful to do everything written in it. Then you will be prosperous and successful."*

It is my responsibility for me to become successful. It's no one else's responsibility, but mine. I cannot blame anyone or keep making excuses as to why I cannot seem to catch a break. No one was or is stopping me. When I became enlightened, I began to shift my attitude and work my faith. I had to stop feeling sorry for myself and start to live my dreams. I learned from that life trial that I had to get to that point to shift my thinking and become a winner instead of a person that's unhappy and always complaining about what's not happening!

Anything in your life that you resolve in yourself to do, will be tested. Have you ever started a diet and the moment you do that's when the boss buys everyone lunch? Or, you have a coworker who has a birthday and one of the other co-workers brings in a big cake? Or when you're determined to work out, that's when it seems like your personal schedule becomes so full, that you seem not to have enough time. However, before then, you had all the time in the world! So, if you know about these tricks and tactics, you can better prepare yourself. When you pass the test, the victory is so much sweeter!

#THE DEATH OF AN ICON
~ Dr. Myles Munroe

I was saddened and heart-broken with the announcement of the tragic death of a great man, the late Dr. Myles Munroe, the Senior Pastor and Founder of the Bahamas Faith Ministries, International. It was a true wake up call to me that tomorrow truly is not promised to you! I heard the news and raced to my computer, trying to pull up articles about this tragedy and searching Google to find out if the reports were true. As I began to realize we had lost a great leader, I began to watch some of his latest sermons and his interviews on Youtube. As he talked about purpose and potential, it stirred something in me. It was though he was waiting for me to play the videos to deliver a message straight to me.

From that day forward, I no longer allowed excuses and fear to stop my progress. I realized I had many stories to tell and businesses to build. I have prolonged certain things, waiting for it to be a perfect time. Guess what? I found out there is no such thing as the perfect time! Time does not care about perfect timing. It's job is to keep going, not waiting on anything. So, I want to convey this to you. Stop waiting on the perfect time. Start with what you have.

The Bible states that a boy had two fishes and five loaves of bread. Jesus blessed it, broke it, and it became more than enough to get the job done. What you have in you is more than enough to get the job done! Big things have the ability to hide in small places. Who would have known that a small African- American preacher by the name of Dr. Martin Luther King, Jr. would have a Civil Rights Movement locked up inside him? He was small in the physical, but his words were mighty! Thousands gathered at his "I Have a Dream" speech. During the Civil Rights Movement, there was no internet or commercial advertising this event. However, thousands were in attendance. I know Dr. Munroe and his Wife, Ruth, are in a better place. His legacy will live on. His impact will continue to be felt.

You have a legacy living in you. Don't die with your legacy unfulfilled. Don't get to the end of your life filled with regrets, only to see someone else create an invention or an idea that came to you first. You would have to watch them enjoy the fruits of what you should have enjoyed.

Sometimes life happens and things blind our view. You have to ask yourself, "Where's The Faith?" Sometimes, we forget how strong we are and what are our capabilities. It is my intention to boost your faith to believe what God has put in you, knowing that the world would benefit from the treasure that He has put in you. There are many battles to be fought, but through faith all things are possible! Now let's go out and win!

#COLD CAR NO HEAT

This place can seem so cold, confusing and downright cruel. You can turn on the news and see riots all over, people crying for justice, and even some crying because of injustice. In our own strength we are so very limited, but with God, we become limitless. I know what you're probably thinking. "What in the world does this have to do with the title of this chapter entitled, "Cold Car with No Heat"? Okay let me explain.

One day, I was at the office. I began to converse with a fellow worker about different situations that were personally going on in our lives. It was not, however, a depressing conversation. It was a conversation about being comfortable with being uncomfortable.

Let me make it clearer for you. Have you ever felt like you came to a point in your life where it didn't matter what decision you made, more than likely any decision you made would have been the wrong decision? No matter how hard you work or what you do, it just turns to nothing, but a pile of frustrations. Plans fall apart, friends walk away and sometimes, the dog don't like you all that much. I can say with certainty, that all of us have come to that point! As my friend and I talked, he stated that he understood where I was coming from concerning the title of this chapter, because it's winter and his car does not have heat. He began to explain that his car malfunctioned and his heater stopped working properly.

Now, if anyone is familiar with Michigan's weather, you know that you're in big trouble if you don't have heat in your car. Last years' temperatures reached, at times, twenty degrees below zero. It was like the Polar Vortex, which is what Michigan residents named it. He felt that since he had purposed to do everything right, that he shouldn't have to struggle so much. He is a pretty hard worker, even was promoted on his job. He has a lovely family and, to the outside person, would seem like a person to model. Obviously, he did not have the financial means to get the repairs done to his vehicle. It's sometimes mind boggling how life's circumstances leave us in a position to trust a higher power.

When we don't have the answers and don't know what to do, we are in a vulnerable state. However, when we lean and depend upon God, he makes us invulnerable! St. John 16:33 says, *"I have told you these things, so that in me you may have [perfect] peace and confidence. In the world you have tribulation and trials and distress and frustration; but be of good cheer [take courage; be confident, certain, undaunted]! For I have overcome the world. [I have deprived it of power to harm you and have conquered it for you.] "*

I really want to make a declaration! Nothing in this world can harm you! That's right!

Nothing! I don't care what it looks like, whether it's your bills, your business sinking, marital problems, or your children not behaving correctly, and even relationship issues. When we have things that are up against us, we have to learn how to trust someone who is higher than we are.

#TRUST

I almost avoided talking about this topic. This is so needed and much can be said about the topic of trust. I will not make this long, but I will give just enough so that you can understand the purpose of trust. Trust is something that seems to be lacking in our society, as a whole. Trust is even lacking in a lot of our personal lives. People definitely don't trust the government anymore. They don't trust politicians, bank officials, and especially, hardly anyone trusts Wall Street. Salesman of any kind, no matter what they are selling, seem to have a target on their backs saying, "Here I am to SELL, SELL, SELL. I am here to sell you something you don't really need!" They are always looked at as people who talk really fast and only want your money.

People especially don't trust our judicial system! As you can see spread all over the news recently, people are crying out. They are coming from a place of distrust! A lack of trust is a trend that is ever interwoven in our society. Am I saying we should trust everybody? No, not at all. I think when we never give new opportunities or new people a chance, we rob ourselves of opportunities and new friendships because we automatically tie them to what happened in the past. We have had some bad experiences. We have seen things and automatically assume it's going to be like what we experienced in the past. That's why when a person comes from an abusive relationship, and they find the courage to leave, they always find it difficult to maintain new relationships. They still have the mindset that they will be abused. No matter how nice the person is and how much they love them, they will always find some way to sabotage the relationship.

This happens, most times, because they have made dysfunction their normal way of doing things. You may have grown up in a home where all you heard was, "You are nothing! You are lazy! You're too fat! You're not good enough!"

Maybe, you grew up with positive reinforcements in life and now you are getting knocked around by life. You are beginning to think what you were told is full of crap. We cannot allow past experiences to rob us of our future. If we are going to accomplish anything in life, we must trust. If you want to have a successful business, you must trust employees. If you want a successful marriage, you must trust your spouse. Any level of success takes trust, because no one can be successful alone.

I mentioned earlier that we can become comfortable with the uncomfortable. Many times, trusting people can be very uncomfortable. You have to depend on them, to an extent. I attended a workshop for leadership training a few years ago. We participated in an exercise where we had to blindfold our partner and lead them down and obstacle course.

Many of the people who were blinded folded were growing very frustrated in the process. They were getting beat up pretty badly from things. They were stepping on and even bumping into walls. One lady was in tears and almost stopped, all together. She wanted to yank the blindfold off because she was growing tired of counting on her leader to feed her specific details on how to avoid traps.

In life, we have many obstacles to overcome. We must put our trust in God, who loves us enough to lead us down the obstacle course of life. Trust is not always easy and is not always comfortable. However, it is necessary. Proverbs 3:5-6, states, *"Lean on, trust in, and be confident in the Lord with all your heart and mind and do not rely on your own insight or understanding. In all your ways know, recognize, and acknowledge Him, and He will direct and make straight and plain your paths."*

#CONCLUSION

I hope you received, at least, a kernel or a morsel of wisdom. If you did, apply them. I can tell you that, if I exhausted all the topics in this one book, it would have likely have been above a thousand pages. It probably would not sell a lot of copies because it was so long. But, I gave you enough to hopefully spark a fire in you to go out and make the necessary changes, thereby creating a positive effect in your life.

In the beginning of the book, I expressed to you where I started. I can say, though, I am not where I started. I will never get to a point where I am satisfied with not growing and neither should you.

Through this journey, my wife and I have learned a lot, prayed a lot, and cried a lot. Please know, that without tribulations, there would not have been growth. I have learned so much from trouble. There is one thing about life, it can be one heck of a teacher. We have lost much, but gained so much more. Now, years later, we have been blessed with so much. Everything we've lost, God has been giving it back in excess!

I am so very happy for those of you who decided to pick up and read this book or listen by audio. I hope that you were encouraged and enlightened. I am a very transparent person. I have opened up a lot about my personal life with the hopes of you learning something new and exciting. My intention is, and has always been, to inspire and uplift people from all walks of life, helping shine a light in this place we call earth.

Continue pressing and moving forward, no matter what life throws at you. Remember, with God all things are possible. The next time you are in a situation ask yourself WTF?!? (Where's The Faith?)